dim sum

dim sum

delicious asian finger food

fiona smith

photography by william lingwood

RYLAND
PETERS
& SMALL

LONDON NEW YORK

Dedication

For Noel Roydhouse and Matthew Macauley

Senior Designer	Louise Leffler
Commissioning Editor	Elsa Petersen-Schepelern
Editors	Maddalena Bastianelli
	Susan Stuck
Production	Patricia Harrington
Art Director	Gabriella Le Grazie
Publishing Director	Alison Starling
Food Stylist	Fiona Smith
Stylist	Helen Trent
Photographer's Assistant	Louise Oliver

Author's acknowledgments

My thanks to Clare Ferguson and Linda Tubby for being such great teachers. Also to Louise Paul, Rebecca Townsend, Marieke Zieleman, Elsa Petersen-Schepelern, and especially my mother, Naomi Roydhouse, who inspired and encouraged me with her own passion for good food. Many thanks also to London's Conran Shop, Nicole Farhi Home Store, Thomas Goode, and Vessel for the beautiful props.

Notes

Specialty Asian ingredients are available in supermarkets, Chinese, Japanese, Thai, and Vietnamese stores.

The choice of oil is important in Asian cooking. Peanut oil can be heated to a very high temperature without burning. It does not have a pronounced flavor. Canola and safflower oil are also suitable. Avoid oils labeled simply "vegetable oil."

First published in United States in 2001
by Ryland Peters & Small Inc.
5th Floor, 519 Broadway
New York, NY10012
www.rylandpeters.com

10 9 8 7 6 5 4 3 2 1
Text © Fiona Smith 2001
Design and photographs © Ryland Peters & Small 2001
Printed and bound in China
ISBN 1 84172 149 2
A catalog record for this book is available from the Library of Congress.

contents

Dim sum is Chinese for "heart's delight"…

Dim sum means "heart's delight" and these heart's delights are the tiny dishes that make up the great yum cha lunches served in Chinese restaurants around the world. Yum cha means "drink tea," but there is a good deal more to it than tea. Diners are offered their choice of delicacies from trolleys piled high with steaming bamboo baskets, plates, and bowls, all holding a mouthwatering array of bite-size dim sum.

Yum cha itself began a little over a hundred years ago in the Chinese province of Canton, gradually spread to Hong Kong, then to other parts of the world. Nowadays there is hardly a Chinatown anywhere that lacks one of the huge, bustling yum cha palaces.

Dim sum include amazing treats such as crisp wontons, potsticker dumplings, spring rolls, noodle wraps, pickled vegetables, steamed buns, and the incomparable Chinese custard tarts.

In this book, I would like to share with you some of the best traditional dim sum—and lots of modern variations. I haven't stopped at China—I'd also like you to try similar dishes inspired by the street food of Thailand, Vietnam, Malaysia, and Japan.

Dim sum partying

Dim sum make marvelous party food, suitable for serving at large parties or as pre-dinner snacks with drinks, or even as appetizers for a dinner party.

Making dim sum yourself might appear daunting because of their sheer variety, but they are in fact simple to make. You can prepare most ingredients in advance, then assemble them at the last minute. I have described advance preparation wherever possible.

Many recipes can be frozen, so it's a good idea to keep some in the freezer. (Those suitable for freezing are marked "F.") Others, like steamed dumplings, can be prepared in bulk, then cooked and served in the same steamer. Keep people's palates interested by using different cooking methods, such as steaming, frying, or baking, then serve others fresh or cold.

Asian ingredients and utensils

Many of the ingredients in this book can be bought in supermarkets, but if you have an Asian market where you live, this is a great place for finding unusual ingredients and also new ideas for serving. Bamboo steamers, for example, are designed to stack up on top of each other so you can cook large amounts at once—and they also make attractive serving dishes.

For parties, try leaves such as banana, lotus, or bamboo to use as liners for plates, trays, and serving dishes, and there are all sorts of inexpensive but stylish bowls, spoons, and chopsticks available too.

Dim sum are modern, fun to prepare and easy to eat—always a big hit at any party.

Dramatic yet simple, these chips are always a hit at a party and can be prepared the day before and stored in an airtight container. Wonton wrappers, also known as "skins," can be used whole or cut in half. They are delicious served with this creamy sweet chile dip. For a low-fat dip, use puréed low-fat cottage cheese or drained nonfat plain yogurt.

black and white sesame wonton chips

¼ cup white sesame seeds
¼ cup black sesame seeds
1–2 packages small wonton wrappers*
sea salt
peanut oil, for frying

Dipping sauce
½ cup Sweet Chile Sauce (page 62)
½ cup crème fraîche or sour cream

Makes 50–60

Packages vary, but contain about 40 large (4 inch) or 70 small (3 inch) wrappers. Leftovers can be frozen.

Fill a large wok or saucepan one-third full with the oil and heat to 375°F, or until a small cube of bread turns golden brown in 30 seconds.

Mix the 2 types of sesame seeds together in a bowl and fill a second small bowl with water. Lay 5 wonton wrappers on a dry surface, brush with water, and sprinkle with seeds. Add the wonton wrappers to the hot oil and fry for 30 seconds until puffed and golden brown. Drain on crumpled paper towels and sprinkle with salt. Repeat until all the wonton wrappers are used.

To make the dipping sauce, mix the Sweet Chile Sauce with the crème fraîche or sour cream, then pour into a serving bowl.

vegetables

These favorite dumplings are browned and steamed in a pan directly over the heat, so they tend to "stick to the pot." The invention of nonstick pans has resolved this problem. Food writer Clare Ferguson first showed me how to make these with pork filling and I now serve this version to vegetarian guests.

Put the dried shiitakes in a bowl, cover with warm water, and let soak for about 30 minutes until softened. Drain, reserving the soaking liquid, and chop the mushrooms finely.

Put the mushrooms in a large bowl. Add the cilantro, garlic, ginger, scallions, chiles, daikon, carrots, bell pepper, and tofu and stir.

Mix the peanut butter and soy sauce in a small bowl or cup, then gently stir into the vegetable mixture.

Put 1 dumpling wrapper on a dry work surface and put 1 level tablespoon of filling in the center. Brush the edge with water and fold into a half-moon shape, pleating one side 3–5 times as you go. Press firmly to seal.

Put on a tray lined with wax paper, flattening the bottom of the dumpling as you do. Repeat with the remaining wrappers and filling, covering with a damp cloth as each one is completed.

Heat a large, preferably nonstick, skillet and brush with 1 teaspoon of the oil. Add as many dumplings as you can in the pan without over-crowding them. Sauté for 2–3 minutes until browned on the bottom.

Mix the reserved mushroom soaking liquid with the stock and pour about ½ cup over the dumplings until part-covered. Bring to a boil, reduce to a simmer, cover, and cook for about 8–10 minutes, until the liquid is absorbed and the dumplings are a little translucent. Repeat with the remaining dumplings.

Serve with the Sweet and Sour Sesame Sauce and cilantro leaves.

15–20 dried shiitake mushrooms

a large bunch of cilantro, including the roots and stems if possible, all finely chopped, about 2 cups

2 garlic cloves, crushed

1 inch fresh ginger, peeled and finely chopped

4 scallions, chopped

1–2 green chiles, seeded and chopped

½ cup peeled and grated daikon radish

2 carrots, peeled and grated, about 1 cup

1 red bell pepper, seeded and finely chopped, about ½ cup

1 cup firm tofu, rinsed, patted dry and chopped into ⅛-inch squares

½ cup crunchy peanut butter

¼ cup dark soy sauce

1 package fresh round dumpling wrappers*

1 tablespoon peanut oil

1–1½ cups vegetable stock

To serve

Sweet and Sour Sesame Sauce (page 63)

a bunch of cilantro, leaves only

Makes 30–36 (F: can be frozen before cooking)

Packages usually contain about 30–36 wrappers. They are kept in the refrigerator in Chinese foodstores.

pot sticker dumplings with peanuts, tofu, and vegetables

1 small red bell pepper

1 small yellow bell pepper

10 asparagus spears, trimmed

10 pieces purple sprouting broccoli or 1 head of broccoli divided into
  florets (or extra asparagus spears)

5 baby eggplants, halved

1 cup fresh shiitake or oyster mushrooms, or enoki mushrooms,
  divided into 10 pieces

peanut or safflower oil, for frying

Crisp batter

1 egg, separated

1 tablespoon lemon juice

⅓ cup all-purpose flour

Roasted salt and pepper

¼ cup sea salt flakes or crystals

4 teaspoons Szechuan peppercorns

Makes about 50

Vegetables cooked in a light, crisp batter are popular all over the world, from the fritto misto of Italy to the tempura of Japan. Make sure the oil is at the right temperature or the batter will be greasy. These are at their most delicious straight from the pan, so serve them at small parties, as part of a lunch, or as a appetizer.

To make the roasted salt and pepper, put the sea salt and Szechuan peppercorns in a small skillet and cook over a low heat for 3–4 minutes until smoking and aromatic. Using a spice grinder or mortar and pestle, lightly crush to a coarse powder. Set aside.

Slice each pepper lengthwise into strips and remove the seeds. Arrange all the vegetables on a platter ready for cooking.

Fill a large wok or saucepan one-third full with the oil and heat to 350°F, or until a small cube of bread turns golden in 45 seconds.

To make the batter, put the egg yolk, lemon juice, and ⅔ cup ice water in a bowl. Beat gently, then beat in the flour to form a smooth batter. Do not overmix.

Beat the egg white in a second bowl until stiff but not dry, then fold into the batter.

Dip each piece of vegetable into the batter, then fry for 3–4 minutes until golden and crisp. Drain on crumpled paper towels. Cook about 10 pieces at a time and bring the oil back to temperature between each batch.

Serve on a platter with piles of the roasted salt and pepper for dipping.

crisp vegetables with roasted salt and pepper dip

Egg fried rice is a popular Chinese dish and Japanese sushi makes excellent party food. I mixed the two together in this dish. Make these rolls in the morning and keep them chilled until 30 minutes before serving.

1 cup Chinese glutinous rice or Japanese sushi rice*

1 teaspoon salt

1 teaspoon sugar

2 teaspoons white rice vinegar

½ cup firm tofu

1 garlic clove, crushed

1 inch fresh ginger, peeled and grated

2 tablespoons light soy sauce

2 tablespoons Sweet Chile Sauce (page 62)

2 tablespoons peanut oil

6 eggs, beaten

6 asparagus spears or 12 green beans, cooked

3 scallions, halved lengthwise

Soy and Ginger Sauce (page 62), to serve

Makes 24

Glutinous rice is sold in Asian foodstores. If unavailable, sushi rice can be used—or even short-grain rice.

Pour 2 cups water into a medium saucepan, bring to a boil, then add the rice and salt. Reduce the heat to a low simmer, cover and cook for 12 minutes without lifting the lid. Remove from the heat and let stand for 5 minutes. Put the sugar and vinegar in a small bowl or cup, stir to dissolve, then mix into the rice. Let cool.

Cut the tofu into ⅛-inch slices. Arrange in a single layer in a flat dish. Put the garlic, ginger, soy, and Sweet Chile Sauce in a small pitcher, mix well, then pour over the tofu. Set aside for 10 minutes.

Heat 1 tablespoon of the oil in a large skillet, add the tofu, and cook for 1½ minutes on each side. Remove from the pan, cut the slices into ⅛-inch strips, then set aside.

Heat 1 teaspoon of the remaining oil in the same skillet and add one-third of the beaten egg. Swirl the egg around to cover the base of the skillet and cook for 2 minutes until set. Carefully remove the omelet to a plate and cook the remaining egg mixture in 2 batches.

Stretch a piece of plastic wrap (about 4 inches longer than your omelet) on a flat surface and put 1 omelet in the middle. Spread with one-third of the rice. Close to the near edge, arrange a line of tofu, asparagus or beans, and scallions—use one-third of the ingredients for each roll. Carefully roll up the omelet, pulling away the plastic as you go. Wrap in the plastic until ready to serve.

Unwrap the rolls and slice into 1-inch pieces. Serve with Soy and Ginger Sauce.

egg rolls with chile tofu

sweet and sour pickled vegetables

1 small cucumber, about 8 inches long

2 carrots

6 radishes, trimmed

3½ inches fresh ginger, peeled

¼ Chinese or Savoy cabbage

3 tablespoons salt

6 dried red chiles (optional)

⅔ cup sugar

2 cups white rice vinegar

¼ cup Shao Hsing (Chinese rice wine), (optional)

1 quart canning jar with lid, sterilized

Makes 3 cups

Cut the cucumber in half lengthwise and scoop out the seeds with a teaspoon. Slice the cucumber, carrots, radishes. and ginger lengthwise into fine strips*.

Slice the cabbage into ½-inch strips and blanch for 30 seconds in boiling water, then drain and rinse with cold water.

Put the cucumber, carrots, and radishes in a shallow glass or china dish and sprinkle with salt. Let stand for 10 minutes, then pat thoroughly dry with paper towels.

Put all the vegetables, ginger, and dried chiles, if using, into a sterilized jar.

Put the sugar, vinegar, and Shao Hsing, if using, into a medium saucepan and bring to a boil, stirring constantly. Reduce the heat and simmer for 10 minutes. Remove from the heat and let cool.

When cool, pour over the vegetables and seal the jar. The pickles will keep in the refrigerator for 2 weeks. The cabbage will discolor after 2 days, but still tastes good.

*Note: Use a mandoline to slice the vegetables; it makes the job easier and gives a more even result. (Inexpensive plastic Japanese mandolines are sold in kitchen stores and Asian markets.)

In Chinese restaurants, the dim sum trolley holds a myriad of exciting tastes and smells and each should be appreciated individually. Chinese pickles are a wonderful way of cleansing the palate between bites. They also make a great accompaniment to many meat and fish dishes. Serve with a jar of chopsticks so guests can help themselves or serve small portions wedged into joined wooden chopsticks (the disposable kind).

Jicama is a round, tan-colored root vegetable with crunchy white flesh, not unlike a water chestnut. It originated in Mexico, where it is still popular, and was introduced to China 300 years ago. If unavailable, use cucumber, green papaya, or Chinese cabbage.

finely grated zest of 1 lime and the juice of 2–3 limes, about ¼ cup

2 teaspoons raw sugar

1 tablespoon light soy sauce

1 tablespoon sesame oil

1 tablespoon grated fresh ginger

2 jicamas, 1 green papaya, 1 long cucumber, or ½ Chinese cabbage

2 romaine lettuce hearts, leaves separated (optional)

Serves 20

Put the lime juice and zest, brown sugar, soy sauce, sesame oil, and ginger in a small jar or bowl and mix well.

If using jicamas, peel and cut into matchsticks. If using papaya, peel with a vegetable peeler, halve, seed, then cut into matchsticks. If using cucumber, cut it in quarters lengthwise, seed, then cut into matchsticks. If using Chinese cabbage, finely shred it.

Just before serving, toss the jicama and dressing together. Serve as a side salad or, at parties, serve it in sake cups or in small romaine lettuce leaves. Arrange on a platter and serve.

jicama and lime salad

Use unroasted, unsalted peanuts, then roast and season them yourself for a clean, fresh flavor. Typical Southeast Asian ingredients are combined in this simple, delicious dish, based on the Indonesian classic salad gado-gado, with its spicy peanut sauce.

⅓ cup fresh peanuts

2 tablespoons peanut oil

4 scallions, chopped

1 fresh red chile, finely chopped

1 tablespoon light soy sauce

1 tablespoon white rice vinegar

1 tablespoon sesame oil

2 cups bean sprouts, trimmed

2 romaine lettuce hearts, leaves
   separated (optional)

Serves 20

Spread the peanuts in a single layer on a baking tray and cook in a preheated oven at 375°F for 15 minutes. Tip the hot nuts onto a clean cloth, fold the sides in so none can escape, then rub vigorously to remove the skins. Transfer the skinned nuts to a board and chop coarsely.

Heat the oil in a wok or skillet over medium heat, add the scallions and chile, and stir-fry for 2 minutes. Add the soy sauce, rice vinegar and sesame oil and heat through.

Remove from the heat and toss in the bean sprouts and peanuts. Serve immediately as a side salad or, at parties, serve it in sake cups or in small romaine lettuce leaves. Arrange on a platter and serve.

wilted bean sprout and peanut salad

These delicate packages—with a hint of green herb and a pink cloud of salmon showing through translucent rice paper wrappers—are a modern update on a Chinese classic. Serving with Asian pesto also gives them a new twist. You could substitute any white fish fillets for the salmon.

salmon and asian pesto packages

To make the pesto, put all the ingredients in a small food processor and grind to a fairly smooth paste. Alternatively, use a mortar and pestle.

Cut the salmon into 20 pieces, about 2 inches square.

Dip a rice paper wrapper in warm water to soften, put a cilantro leaf in the center, then top with a piece of salmon and a teaspoon of pesto. Fold in the sides to form a neat square (trim the edges if the wrapper is too big). The damp wrappers will stick closed.

Heat the oil in a skillet and cook the parcels, in batches, sealed side down, for 3 minutes until brown.*

Transfer them to a steamer set over boiling water and steam for 4–6 minutes. Serve on their own, or with a Sweet Chile or Soy and Ginger dipping sauce.

*Note: The packages can be made and fried ahead of time, covered with plastic wrap, chilled and steamed when needed, or cooked in advance and served cold.

1½ lb. skinless salmon fillets
20 dry rice paper wrappers*
a small bunch of cilantro, leaves only
1 tablespoon peanut oil
Sweet Chile or Soy and Ginger Sauce
  (pages 62–63), to serve

Asian pesto
4 garlic cloves, crushed
½ cup cashews, chopped
a large bunch of cilantro, leaves only
a large bunch of Thai basil or ordinary basil, leaves only
⅓ cup peanut oil
sea salt flakes, to taste

Makes 20 (F: if using fresh salmon, the packages may be frozen before cooking)

Vietnamese rice paper wrappers are available in various diameters, ranging from 6–8 inches. All are suitable for this recipe.

fish and seafood

If using fresh squid, you will need to clean it: first: pull the tentacles out of the body, then cut off the rosette of tentacles—you may need to press out the tiny hard piece from the middle of the rosette. Keep the tentacles and bodies and discard the rest. Pull the quill (the transparent "spine") out of the body and discard it. You can remove the thin purplish skin if you like, but I think it tastes good. Rinse the bodies, pat dry, and cut lengthwise into 4–6 strips.

Put the breadcrumbs, garlic, ginger, parsley, chiles, 5-spice, and salt in a bowl and mix well. Mix the egg and soy sauce in a second bowl.

Fill a wok or saucepan one-third full with the oil and heat to 350°F, or until a small cube of bread turns golden in 45 seconds. Dust the squid with flour, dip into the egg, then the breadcrumb mixture. Fry in batches of 8 for 2–3 minutes, then remove and drain on crumpled paper towels. Keep them warm while you cook the remainder.

Serve with Sweet and Sour Sesame or Sweet Chile Sauce.

6–8 medium (6–8 inches) squid, about 1 lb.
¾ cup fresh breadcrumbs
2 garlic cloves, crushed
1 inch fresh ginger, peeled and grated
a small bunch of parsley, finely chopped
2 fresh red or green chiles, finely chopped
2 teaspoons 5-spice powder
1 teaspoon salt
2 eggs, beaten
2 tablespoons soy sauce
peanut oil, for frying
flour, for dusting
Sweet and Sour Sesame or Sweet Chile Sauce (pages 62–63), to serve

Makes 32

spicy crumbed squid strips

I always use fresh squid, but you can also buy it frozen, either whole or cleaned—though if they're cleaned, they won't have their pretty flowerlike tentacles. Squid, octopus, and cuttlefish are some of the few ingredients that are equally good, if not better, after being frozen—freezing serves the same purpose as the fisherman beating the fish against a stone to tenderize it.

1 lb. skinned, boneless white fish fillets, such as cod

6 scallions, finely chopped

1 inch fresh ginger, peeled and grated

1 small can (3 oz.) bamboo shoots, drained and
  chopped

1 tablespoon shrimp paste or oyster sauce

1 egg white, beaten

2 teaspoons sesame oil

½ teaspoon salt

½ teaspoon white pepper

24 large wonton wrappers*

peanut oil, for frying

Sweet and Sour Sesame or Sweet Chile Sauce
  (pages 62–63), to serve

Makes 24

*Packages vary, but contain about 40 large (4 inch)
or 70 small (3 inch) wonton wrappers (or "skins").
Leftovers can be frozen.*

Fish and shrimp balls are a regular feature in Chinese teahouses, served fried, steamed, or in soup. To obtain the dramatic effect of the wonton coating they must be fried, but they taste delicious however you cook them.

Put the fish, scallions, and ginger in a food processor and process in short bursts until minced, being careful not to overmix. Transfer to a bowl and knead in the chopped bamboo shoots, shrimp paste or oyster sauce, egg white, sesame oil, salt, and pepper. Chill for about 30 minutes or until required.

Using scissors or a sharp knife, shred the wonton wrappers into fine strands. Cover and set aside.

Fill a wok or saucepan one-third full with the oil and heat to 350°F, or until a small cube of bread turns golden in 45 seconds.

With wet hands, divide the fish mixture into 24 even balls. Roll the balls in the shredded wontons. Fry in batches of 4–6 for 4 minutes. Remove with a slotted spoon and drain on crumpled paper towels.

Serve with Sweet and Sour Sesame or Sweet Chile Sauce.

Variations

• Put the balls in a steamer over boiling water and cook for 5 minutes.

• Drop the balls into simmering soup 5 minutes before it is served.

fish balls with shredded wonton coating

Fermented black beans, also known as salty black beans or Chinese black beans, are sold packed in plastic bags in larger supermarkets and Chinese foodstores. Although you could use ready-made black bean sauce, I encourage you to make your own, as it is very simple and makes a world of difference to the flavor.

8 oz. fresh or dried Chinese egg noodles

1 tablespoon sesame oil

24 green-lipped mussels, cooked*

a small bunch of cilantro, chopped

Black bean sauce

1 tablespoon peanut oil

2 garlic cloves, crushed

2 inches fresh ginger, peeled and finely shredded

4 scallions, finely sliced

2 teaspoons cornstarch

2 tablespoons fermented black beans, lightly crushed

Makes 24

In my native New Zealand, these mussels are available fresh. In other parts of the world, they are sold precooked.

Cook the noodles in boiling water until just done, about 3–4 minutes for fresh or 7–9 minutes for dried. Drain and toss in a bowl with the sesame oil.

To make the black bean sauce, heat the peanut oil in a small wok or saucepan, add the garlic, ginger, and scallions and cook for 2 minutes. Put the cornstarch in a small bowl with 1 tablespoon water, stir until smooth, then add enough water to make ½ cup. Add the black beans and cornstarch mixture to the wok. Bring to a boil and stir until thickened, about 2 minutes. Toss with the noodles.

Discard one of each pair of mussel shells, so each mussel sits on its half shell. Loosen the mussel if necessary. Twist a fork into the noodles, taking a small amount to arrange in each mussel shell.

Put the mussels in a steamer over boiling water and heat through for 5 minutes. Scatter with chopped cilantro and serve immediately.

mussels with egg noodles and black bean sauce

shrimp and scallion fritters

These fritters are based on a Mexican original—I've added a Chinese twist. You can fry or sauté them ahead of time then reheat in a 350°F oven for 5 minutes. For a milder taste, use green chiles, and for hotter, use red.

2 eggs

1 tablespoon fish sauce

2 tablespoons Shao Hsing (Chinese rice wine) or
   dry sherry

1 cup plus 2 tablespoons rice flour

8 scallions, diagonally sliced

8 oz. peeled small shrimp, about 1 cup

2 green or red chiles, seeded and finely sliced

peanut oil, for frying or sautéing

Cilantro salsa

a small bunch of fresh cilantro, finely chopped

2 large tomatoes, skinned, seeded, and finely chopped,

1 small red onion, finely chopped

2 tablespoons fish sauce

2 teaspoons sugar

Makes 24

Put the eggs, fish sauce, and Shao Hsing or sherry in a large bowl, add ⅓ cup cold water, and beat well. Beat in the rice flour to form a smooth batter. Let stand for 10 minutes, then stir in the scallions, shrimp, and chiles.

To fry, fill a wok or saucepan one-third full with the oil and heat to 350°F, or until a small cube of bread turns golden in 45 seconds. Drop tablespoonfuls of the mixture into the hot oil and fry for 3 minutes or until golden. Drain on crumpled paper towels.

To sauté, heat 1 tablespoon of the oil in a large skillet. Drop tablespoons of mixture into the skillet and cook for about 2 minutes on each side.

Mix all the salsa ingredients together in a small serving bowl and serve with the fritters. Alternatively, serve by themselves, or with your choice of store-bought or homemade Asian dipping sauces.

pea shoot and shrimp dumplings

Pea shoots are leaf shoots of the snow pea or garden pea. Sold in Chinese supermarkets and some gourmet stores, they taste like essence of peas! Use snow peas if you can't find them. Serve without any dip, so the subtle flavors aren't overpowered.

8 oz. fresh pea shoots or snow peas, chopped, about 2 cups

1 lb. uncooked shrimp, shelled, deveined and coarsely chopped, about 2 cups. prepared

2 inches fresh ginger, peeled and grated

1 tablespoon light soy sauce

1 tablespoon Shao Hsing (Chinese rice wine) or dry sherry (optional)

1 teaspoon sesame oil

1 egg white, beaten

extra fresh pea shoots or Chinese chives, to serve

Rice flour dough

1 cup plus 2 tablespoons all-purpose flour

¾ cup rice flour

2 tablespoons peanut oil

Makes 32

To make the dough, mix the 2 flours in a bowl, then stir in 1 cup boiling water and the oil. Stir until cool enough to handle, then knead to form a smooth mass. Put in a plastic bag and chill for 30 minutes.

Put the pea shoots or snow peas in a colander and pour over boiling water, then quickly refresh under cold running water and set aside.

Put the shrimp in a bowl and mix in the ginger, soy sauce, Shao Hsing or sherry, sesame oil, and egg white. Set aside for 15 minutes to develop the flavors. Add the chopped pea shoots or snow peas.

Divide the dough into 32 pieces, roll into balls, and cover with a damp cloth. Dust a dry surface with flour and, using a rolling pin, roll out a ball of dough to a circle, 3 inches in diameter. Put 1 heaped teaspoon of filling in the center, brush the edges with water, then bring them together to enclose the filling. Twist to seal and break off any excess dough. Repeat until all are made, keeping the dumplings covered as you make them.

Put the dumplings, sealed edge down, in a steamer and steam over boiling water for 7 minutes. Serve with extra pea shoots or chives.

Perfect for parties where you need a more substantial snack. Serve with a selection of sauces and the salads on pages 18–19. You don't even need plates; the banana leaves (or foil) can do that job.

sticky rice in banana leaves with chicken skewers

To make the skewers, cut the chicken into ½-inch cubes and thread onto the presoaked bamboo skewers. Mix the hoisin sauce in a shallow dish or tray with the chile sauce and Shao Hsing or sherry, if using. Add the skewers, turn to coat, then marinate in the refrigerator for at least 2 hours.

Put the rice and chicken stock in a large saucepan and bring to a boil. Cover and simmer for 10 minutes, until partially cooked.

Wash the banana leaves and cut into 6-inch squares. Divide the rice into 12 portions (about 4–5 tablespoons each) and put 1 portion in the middle of each banana leaf or foil square. Top with some red bell pepper, ginger, scallion, and cilantro. Fold in the sides and secure with a toothpick. Steam over boiling water for 10 minutes.

Light an outdoor grill or preheat the broiler. Cook the chicken skewers for 6 minutes on each side. Serve these on the sticky rice with a selection of sauces.

2 cups glutinous (sticky) rice
3 cups chicken stock
3–4 banana leaves, about 6 oz.,
   or 12 pieces foil, 6 inches square
2 red bell peppers, finely sliced
2 inches fresh ginger, peeled and finely
   sliced
2 scallions, sliced lengthwise
a bunch of cilantro
selection of sauces (pages 62–63), to serve

Chicken skewers
2 lb. skinless, boneless chicken breast
½ cup hoisin sauce
2 tablespoons chile sauce
2 tablespoons Shao Hsing (Chinese rice
   wine) or dry sherry (optional)

*24 bamboo skewers, soaked in water
   for 30 minutes*

Makes 12

chicken and duck

Traditionally filled with pork or bean paste, these fluffy buns are a popular and comforting dim sum. For a whiter bun, you can replace half the flour with potato flour, but the dough is less elastic, so harder to handle.

little Szechuan **chicken steamed buns**

Put the chicken in a baking dish. Put the soy sauce in a bowl, mix in the honey, Shao Hsing or sherry, chile sauce, garlic, and peppercorns, add to the chicken and turn to coat. Cover with foil or a lid and marinate for 30 minutes to 2 hours.

Preheat the oven to 350°F. Roast the chicken, still covered, for 20 minutes, then uncover and cook a further 20 minutes. Let cool, remove the meat from the bones, shred finely, and mix with any marinade and juices left in the dish.

To make the dough, put the flour in a large bowl and mix in the baking powder, sugar, and salt. Stir in the milk, oil and 6 tablespoons water to form a dough. Turn the dough onto a floured board and knead for 5 minutes until it becomes elastic. Cover and let it rest at room temperature for about 1 hour.

Divide the dough into 24 pieces and cover with a damp cloth. Take 1 piece of dough and, using your fingers, shape into a 2½-inch disk. Put 1 teaspoon of the chicken filling in the center and gather up the dough around it. Pinch the edges together and twist to seal. Put, sealed edges up, on a square of parchment paper, cover, and repeat with the remaining dough and filling.

Put the buns in a steamer, 1 inch apart, and steam for 15–20 minutes*.

*Note: You can steam the buns the day before, keeping them well wrapped and chilled. Re-steam them for 5 minutes before serving.

4 chicken thighs

3 tablespoons dark soy sauce

2 tablespoons honey

1 tablespoon Shao Hsing (Chinese rice wine) or dry sherry

1–2 tablespoons hot chile sauce

2–3 garlic cloves, crushed

1 tablespoon Szechuan peppercorns, crushed

Fluffy dough

1½ cups all-purpose flour

3 teaspoons baking powder

2 tablespoons sugar

½ teaspoon salt

⅓ cup milk

3 tablespoons peanut oil

24 squares of parchment paper, 2 x 2 inches

Makes 24

These are an incredibly fresh-tasting version of the popular Vietnamese spring rolls. Thai basil has a distinctive spicy taste, reminiscent of aniseed—each of the herbs in this recipe adds its own unique flavor, so try to use all three.

4 skinless, boneless chicken breasts, about 6 oz. each

¼ cup dark soy sauce

2 inches fresh ginger, peeled and grated

2 garlic cloves, crushed

2 tablespoons Shao Hsing (Chinese rice wine) or dry sherry (optional)

24 small rice paper wrappers, 6½ inch diameter

a small bunch of cilantro

a small bunch of mint

a small bunch of Thai basil or ordinary sweet basil

Dipping sauce (optional)

½ cup sugar

grated zest and juice of 2 limes

2 green chiles, finely sliced

⅓ cup white rice vinegar

Makes 24

Put the chicken in an oven cooking bag, add the soy sauce, ginger, garlic, and Shao Hsing or sherry. Knead the bag so the chicken is thoroughly coated. Marinate in the refrigerator for at least 2 hours or overnight.

Preheat the oven to 350°F. Transfer the chicken in the bag to a roasting pan and cook for about 40 minutes. Remove from the oven and let cool in the bag.

Slice each chicken breast diagonally into 12 pieces, put on a plate, and pour over any juices.

To assemble, dip a rice paper wrapper in warm water to soften. Put on a damp surface and top with 2 pieces of chicken and a few leaves of each herb, then wrap up. Repeat until all 24 have been made.

To make the dipping sauce, put all the ingredients in a saucepan and boil for 5 minutes. Transfer to a small bowl and serve with the spring rolls.

three herb and chicken spring rolls

A Southeast Asian version of *sui mai,* a Chinese classic. The Chinese version was taught to me by Clare Ferguson, a legendary party giver. She says they make perfect party food as they freeze well and look gorgeous served straight from bamboo steamers.

steamed dumplings
with kaffir lime and lemongrass

Using a small food processor or large mortar and pestle, grind the garlic, galangal or ginger, lemongrass, kaffir lime leaves, chiles, and shallots to form a paste—add a little of the fish sauce or soy sauce if needed. Transfer to a bowl, add the remaining fish or soy sauce, minced chicken, and coconut cream, and stir well.

Cut the wonton wrappers into rounds and discard the trimmings. Put a wrapper on a dry surface and spread with a teaspoon of filling. Gather up the edges to form a basket shape. Tap this a few times on the work surface to fill in the gathers and put on a tray lined with wax paper. Repeat until all are made, keeping the wrappers and the dumplings covered as you go.*

Steam over boiling water for 8 minutes and serve immediately, with Sweet Chile or Soy and Ginger Sauce.

*Note: To freeze, put on a tray in the freezer until hard, about 1 hour, then put in bags until needed. To cook, put in the steamer and bring to semi-frozen, about 15 minutes. Steam for 12 minutes and serve.

2 garlic cloves, crushed

2 inches fresh galangal or ginger, peeled and finely chopped

2 stalks lemongrass, finely chopped

8 kaffir lime leaves, finely chopped

2 hot Thai chiles, seeded and finely chopped

12 shallots, finely chopped

¼ cup fish sauce or light soy sauce

1 lb. skinless, boneless chicken breast, ground

¼ cup coconut cream

50 small fresh wonton wrappers*

Sweet Chile or Soy and Ginger Sauce (pages 62–63), to serve

Makes 50 (F: can be frozen before cooking)

Packages vary, but contain about 40 large (4-inch) or 70 small (3-inch) wrappers. Leftovers can be frozen.

½ cup long-grain rice

36 large Chinese leaves, such as large bok choy,
    choi sum, or Chinese cabbage, about 1 lb.

1½ cups ground chicken breast, about 12 oz.

6 scallions, chopped

2 garlic cloves, crushed

2 inches fresh ginger, peeled and grated

2 green chiles, seeded and finely chopped

2 teaspoons 5-spice powder

2 tablespoons hoisin or yellow bean sauce

1 small can water chestnuts, 6 oz., drained and chopped

Plum Sauce (page 63), to serve

Makes 36

Boil the rice in salted water for 10 minutes, then drain.

Separate the leaves of the bok choy, choi sum, or cabbage—each should be at least 5 x 3 inches. Blanch in boiling water, then refresh in cold water.

Put the chicken, scallions, garlic, ginger, chiles, 5-spice, hoisin or yellow bean sauce, and water chestnuts in a bowl and mix well.

Put 1 tablespoon of the mixture in the center of each leaf and roll up. Steam for 10 minutes over boiling water, then serve with Plum Sauce.

In Eastern Europe, meat and rice wrapped in cabbage is very popular. The idea also lends itself very well to Chinese ingredients, making perfect dim sum. There are many popular vegetables from the cabbage family in Chinese cuisine—any, as long as the leaves are big enough, are suitable here.

bok choy rolls with spicy chicken

Cooking traditional Peking duck is a time-consuming process involving drying, boiling and basting, not to mention the actual cooking! A much easier option is buying a ready-prepared duck. Another simple solution is to use just the duck breast, which gives a succulent, simple result. These wraps always go down well at parties and are perfect picnic fare. The paper wrappers keep them moist and stop them sticking together if you prepare them in advance. Chinese pancakes are sold by Chinese grocers—find them in the frozen food section or refrigerated case.

Score the duck fat diagonally at ⅛ inch intervals and rub in the salt. Mix the soy sauce, honey, and 5-spice in a flat glass or ceramic dish. Put the duck breasts, skin side up, in the marinade, moving them about so the flesh is coated. Marinate in the refrigerator for at least 2 hours.

Remove the duck from the marinade and pat dry with paper towels.

Heat the oil in a skillet, add the duck breasts, skin side down, and cook for 8 minutes. Pour off the fat from the skillet, then turn the breasts and cook the other side for 4 minutes. Let cool. Slice each duck breast diagonally into 6 strips.

Quarter the cucumber lengthwise and scoop out and discard the seeds. Slice each quarter in 6 lengthwise and then in half crosswise. You should have 48 pieces.

To assemble, steam the pancakes for 5 minutes over boiling water. When filling, work on 3–4 pancakes at a time and keep the others covered so they don't dry out. Spread 1 teaspoon of hoisin sauce on each pancake, add a piece of duck, a few strips of cucumber, and a piece of scallion. Fold up the bottom, then the sides. Wrap the pieces of paper around the pockets in the same way, then cover with a cloth until ready to serve. Serve alone or with Sweet Chile Sauce.

4 duck breasts, 6 oz. each
1 tablespoon salt
¼ cup dark soy sauce
1 tablespoon honey
2 teaspoons 5-spice powder
1 tablespoon peanut oil

To serve

1 cucumber, about 12 inches long
24 Chinese pancakes
½ cup hoisin sauce
6 scallions, halved lengthwise and crosswise
Sweet Chile Sauce (page 63)

24 squares of parchment paper, 5 x 5 inches

Makes 24

peking-style duck pancake wraps

Chile beef makes a great filling for wontons, which are more traditionally filled with minced pork and shrimp. They can be fried in advance and reheated in a 375°F oven for about 8 minutes before serving.

To make the filling, slice the steak into thin strips and, if they are wider than ½ inch, slice them in half lengthwise. Put in a bowl and mix in the sesame oil, vinegar, and oyster sauce.

Using a small food processor or mortar and pestle, grind the chiles, ginger, garlic, and salt to a coarse paste. Add to the steak, mix well, and set aside for about 30 minutes.

Put 1 tablespoon of filling in the center of each wonton wrapper, brush around the edges with the egg white, and gather up, twisting to seal.

Fill a wok or skillet one-third full with the oil and heat to 375°F or until a small cube of bread turns golden brown in 30 seconds. Cook the wontons in batches of 6 for 2–3 minutes until golden and crisp. Drain on paper towels, then serve with one of the sauces.

1 lb. sirloin steak
1 tablespoon sesame oil
2 teaspoons white rice vinegar
3 tablespoons oyster sauce
2–4 fresh red chiles, seeded and chopped
2 inches fresh ginger, peeled and chopped
3 garlic cloves
1 teaspoon salt
32 large wonton wrappers*
1 egg white, beaten
peanut oil, for frying
Sweet and Sour Sesame or Plum Sauce (pages 62–63), to serve

Makes 32 (F: the wontons can be frozen before cooking)

*Packages vary, but contain about 40 large (4-inch) or 70 small (3-inch) wrappers. Leftovers can be frozen.

crisp chile beef wontons

meat

This dim sum is one of my favorites. Succulent pieces of meat are steamed in their own sauce—I find marinating and cooking them in the same oven cooking bag saves a lot of mess and washing up. Unless you own a particularly large cleaver, get your butcher to chop the ribs for you.

2 lb. pork spareribs, cut into
    2-inch pieces
½ cup hoisin sauce
2 garlic cloves, crushed
2 inches fresh ginger, peeled and grated
6 scallions, sliced
2 tablespoons Shao Hsing (Chinese rice
    wine) or dry sherry
2 tablespoons Chinese black beans,
    crushed (optional), *see* page 27
toasted sesame seeds, to serve

Makes about 48

Put all the ingredients except the sesame seeds in an oven cooking bag or ovenproof dish, mix well, seal or cover with foil, and marinate for at least 2 hours or overnight in the refrigerator.

Preheat the oven to 350°F. Cook the spareribs, still in the cooking bag or sealed dish, for 40 minutes. Transfer to warmed serving dishes and sprinkle with the sesame seeds.

mini hoisin spareribs

½ cup white glutinous rice

½ cup black glutinous rice

2 teaspoons salt

1¼ cups ground beef, about 10 oz.

6 oz. fresh shiitake mushrooms, finely chopped, about 1 cup

6 shallots or 1 small onion, finely chopped

2 garlic cloves, crushed

2 inches fresh ginger, peeled and grated

1 egg, beaten

¼ cup mushroom soy sauce or oyster sauce

Sweet and Sour Sesame or Plum Sauce (page 63), to serve (optional)

Makes 32

Put the white and black rice in two separate saucepans, add ½ cup water and 1 teaspoon salt to each, and bring to a boil. Drain immediately and rinse well.

Put the beef in a bowl, add the mushrooms, shallots or onion, garlic, ginger, beaten egg, and soy or oyster sauce, and mix well. Make 32 balls of mixture, about 1 tablespoon each, rolling with wet hands.

Mix the black and white rice together, then roll the meatballs in the rice so they are well coated.

Line a steamer with parchment paper and arrange the pearl balls about 1 inch apart. Steam for 30 minutes until the rice is cooked.

Serve alone or with Sweet and Sour Sesame or Plum Sauce.

This dim sum goes under many names, including "lion's head," "porcupine," and "pearl"—all because of the grains of rice sticking to the outside of the meatball. This recipe calls for black and white glutinous rice, but if black is unavailable, just white is fine.

two-rice pearl balls

Chicken stock

8 oz. chicken pieces, such as wings and thighs

2 inches fresh ginger, peeled and sliced

3 garlic cloves

1 onion, halved

a large bunch of parsley or cilantro

4 whole star anise

sea salt, to taste

Pork and shrimp wontons

1 cup ground pork, about 8 oz.

6 scallions, chopped

¼ cup light soy sauce

Wonton soup is a wonderful Chinese classic and if you thought it had no place at a dim sum party, you would be wrong. Serve each wonton with a dash of hot soup in the little china or plastic spoons you can find in any Asian supermarket. In bowls, this soup serves 4–6.

pork and shrimp wonton soup with wilted lettuce

1 cup small uncooked shrimp, shelled and deveined

32 small wonton wrappers*

1 romaine lettuce heart, shredded

Makes 32 (F: the wontons can be frozen before cooking)

Packages vary, but contain about 40 large (4-inch) or 70 small (3-inch) wrappers. Leftovers can be frozen.

Put all the stock ingredients except the salt into a large saucepan. Add 8 cups water, bring to a boil, reduce to a simmer and cook for 45 minutes, skimming off any foam that rises to the surface. Strain. Remove any meat from the chicken bones, shred it, and return it to the stock. Taste and adjust the seasoning.

To make the wontons, mix the pork, scallions, and soy sauce in a bowl. Cut the shrimp in 2 or 3, to give 32 even pieces.

Brush the edges of each wonton wrapper with water and spread 1 heaped teaspoon of filling in the center. Top with a piece of shrimp. Gather the edges and twist and pinch them around the filling to seal.

Bring the stock to a boil and drop in the wontons. Cook for about 3–5 minutes until the wontons rise to the surface.

Put a few shreds of lettuce in each spoon, add a wonton, and some soup and serve immediately.*

*Note: To keep the soup as hot as possible while serving, preheat the spoons by soaking them in hot water for a few minutes.

You may have eaten this dish in its usual, large form in a restaurant. Reducing the size of the package to a small dim sum makes rice in lotus leaves a far more manageable finger food. Lotus leaves impart wonderful flavor, but if these are unavailable, try to use another fragrant leaf such as banana, pandanus, or grape. Failing this, cabbage will do, but blanch it in boiling water first.

grilled pork and rice in lotus leaves

Put the soy sauce in a large bowl. Add the honey, hoisin sauce, Shao Hsing or sherry, tomato purée or ketchup, and 5-spice powder. Mix well, then add the pork and coat well. Cover and marinate in the refrigerator for up to 4 hours.

Light an outdoor grill or preheat the broiler. Cook the pork for about 6–8 minutes on each side. Wrap the pork in foil and set aside for about 10 minutes. Slice the meat off the bone and mix it with any collected juices and marinade.

Put 3 cups water in a saucepan and bring to a boil. Add the rice and salt and reduce to a simmer. Cover and cook for 12 minutes. Set aside, covered, for 5 minutes.

Soak the lotus leaves in water until soft, about 20 minutes, then cut each leaf into strips about 4 x 8 inches.

Put 1 tablespoon rice and 1 tablespoon pork in each piece of leaf, fold up into a package and secure with a toothpick.

Arrange in a bamboo steamer over a wok or saucepan of boiling water and steam for 10 minutes. Serve.

2 tablespoons dark soy sauce

2 tablespoons honey

2 tablespoons hoisin sauce

2 tablespoons Shao Hsing (Chinese rice wine) or dry sherry (optional)

2 tablespoons tomato purée or ketchup

1 teaspoon 5-spice powder

6 bone-in pork chops, about 2 lb.

1½ cups glutinous rice*

½ teaspoon salt

4 dried lotus leaves or equivalent of banana, pandanus, grape, or blanched cabbage leaves

Makes 24

Glutinous rice is sold in Asian foodstores. If unavailable, sushi rice can be used instead.

These spring rolls are very easy to get on with—they can be made up to the frying stage, then frozen. Cook them from frozen for 4–5 minutes in the hot oil. To make vegetarian spring rolls, replace the pork with an equivalent amount of finely chopped vegetables such as peppers, carrots, zucchini, or mushrooms.

pork, tofu, and broccoli spring rolls

Cut the pork tenderloin into strips ⅛ x ⅛ inch and 1 inch long.

Heat 1 tablespoon of the oil in a wok, add the shallots, garlic, and pork and stir-fry for 2 minutes. Add the broccoli, tofu, oyster sauce, soy sauce, vinegar, and sugar and stir-fry for 2 minutes longer.

Cut the spring roll wrappers into quarters. Put 1 teaspoon of filling at one end. Fold in the sides and roll up, sealing the ends with a little water.

Fill a wok or saucepan one-third full of the oil and heat to 375°F, or until a small cube of bread turns golden brown in 30 seconds. Add the spring rolls in batches of 8 and fry for 3–4 minutes until golden brown. Keep the cooked rolls hot in the oven until all are ready.

Serve with a choice of a hot sauce (Sweet Chile or Sweet and Sour Sesame) and a mild sauce (Soy and Ginger or Plum).

8 oz. pork tenderloin
6 medium shallots, finely chopped
2 garlic cloves, crushed
½ cup broccoli, broken into tiny florets
⅓ cup firm tofu, cut into ⅛-inch dice
2 tablespoons oyster sauce
2 tablespoons dark soy sauce
2 teaspoons white rice vinegar
2 teaspoons sugar
8 large spring roll wrappers
peanut oil, for frying
a selection of sauces, for dipping
   (pages 62–63)

Makes 32 (F: can be frozen before cooking)

The westernized version of the fortune cookie—found all around the world—although good fun, is always a bland, tough thing. The cookie in this recipe is light, crisp, and delicious, and can be wrapped around the fortune of your choice, from the traditional to the hilarious or the personal.

orange and almond fortune cookies

Put the egg whites in a bowl and beat until very stiff. Gently fold in the sugar, almonds, flour, then the cooled butter, orange flower water, if using, and orange zest.

Preheat the oven to 375°F. Spread teaspoonfuls of the mixture very thinly on the baking sheet (4–6 should fit on the sheet). Bake for 6–8 minutes until golden. Working very quickly, fold each cookie in half around a fortune. Cool on a wire rack.

Repeat until all are made. The cookies will keep for up to 1 week in an airtight container.

2 egg whites
⅓ cup sugar
½ cup ground almonds
⅓ cup all-purpose flour, sifted
4 tablespoons butter, melted and cooled
1 teaspoon orange flower water (optional)
finely grated zest of 1 orange

a large baking sheet, lined with
*   parchment paper*
24 small pieces of paper with fortune

Makes 24

sweet things

12 oz. your favorite pie crust dough

1 cup milk

1 cup heavy cream

1 cinnamon stick

4 whole star anise

6 whole cloves

6 pieces licorice root (optional)

4 eggs

¼ cup sugar

1 whole nutmeg

24 2-inch tartlet molds, buttered

3-inch cookie cutter, plain or fluted

Makes 24

five-spice custard tarts

Five-spice powder can be a combination of many spices—Szechuan pepper, cinnamon, cloves, fennel, star anise, cassia, licorice root—all mixed to add flavor to savory dishes. Here, a careful selection of spices makes a wonderful addition to sweet custard tarts, served throughout a yum cha meal.

Roll out the dough to $\frac{1}{16}$-inch thickness and cut out 24 circles with the cookie cutter. Line the prepared molds with the pastry. Chill for about 30 minutes.

Put the milk and cream in a small saucepan and slowly bring to a boil. Add the cinnamon, star anise, cloves, and licorice root, if using. Let infuse off the heat for 30 minutes. Preheat the oven to 350°F.

Put the eggs and sugar in a bowl and beat until pale. Strain the milk mixture over the eggs and beat well.

Pour the filling into the pastry shells and grate a little nutmeg on top. Bake for 15–20 minutes until the custard has set. Remove from the oven and serve cool.

Asian pears, also called Chinese pears or apple pears, can be found in Asian specialty shops and in many supermarkets. They have yellow skin, crisp white flesh, and a long black stem. These little puddings are dim sum size, but this recipe would also make six regular-sized puddings.

steamed pear and ginger puddings

1 stick (½ cup) butter

¾ cup maple syrup or dark corn syrup

3 eggs

2 cups self-rising flour, sifted

3 Asian pears, peeled, cored and finely chopped

¾ cup crystallized ginger, finely chopped

*12 teacups or medium ramekins, ⅔ cup each,
or 18 small, ½ cup each, well buttered*

Makes 12–18

Put the butter and syrup in a large bowl and beat until light and fluffy. Beat in the eggs one at a time. Fold in the flour and then the chopped pears and ginger.

Divide the mixture between the teacups* or ramekins in 2 tiers of a large bamboo steamer, or 3–4 of a medium steamer. Set over a wok or saucepan of simmering water and steam for 30–40 minutes, topping up with boiling water as necessary.

*Note: To prevent the teacups from cracking when used in cooking, they should be tempered before use. Put them on a rack in a saucepan and cover with cold water. Cover with a lid, bring to a boil, and simmer for 10 minutes. Turn off the heat and let cool to room temperature. The cups are now ready for use.

To make the sauce, put the sugar, lime juice and zest, chile flakes, if using, and ½ cup water in a medium saucepan and bring to a boil, stirring until the sugar has dissolved. Simmer for 7 minutes until syrupy. Cool and transfer to a serving bowl.

To make the wontons, slice the flesh off the mangoes and chop into ⅛-inch dice. Heat the butter and sugar in a wok or skillet and stir in the mango. Cook for 1 minute, then let cool.

Put 1 tablespoon of the mango mixture at one corner of each wonton skin. Brush the edges with water, roll up and twist each end so you have a bonbon shape.

Fill a wok or saucepan one-third full of the oil and heat to 375°F or until a small cube of bread turns golden brown in 30 seconds. Fry the wontons in batches of 6 for 1–2 minutes, bringing the oil back to temperature between each batch. Drain on crumpled paper towels.

Serve immediately with the lime dipping sauce.

2 large mangoes, 12 oz. each
2 tablespoons unsalted butter
2 tablespoons natural cane sugar
36 large wonton wrappers*
peanut oil, for frying

Lime sauce
½ cup sugar
juice and grated zest of 2 limes
¼ teaspoon dried chile flakes (optional)

Makes 36

Packages vary, but contain about 40 large (4-inch) or 70 small (3-inch) wrappers. Leftovers can be frozen.

mango wontons with lime sauce

Wonton wrappers can enclose lots of surprises. Mango is a delicious filling, especially with a tangy lime dipping sauce. If you want to be adventurous, add chile—it gives it a real kick!

sweet chile sauce

Sweet Chile Sauce is a favorite Thai accompaniment for chicken, but is also very good with seafood, vegetables, and meat. Use large chiles, rather than the tiny hot bird chiles—they are milder so you can use more and achieve a better-colored sauce.

1¼ cups sugar

1 cup white rice vinegar

3–5 garlic cloves, crushed

4 red chiles, seeded and finely chopped

1 inch fresh ginger, peeled and grated

1 pint canning jar with lid, sterilized

Makes 2 cups

Put the sugar and vinegar in a saucepan and bring to a boil, stirring until the sugar has dissolved.

Simmer for 10 minutes, then add the garlic, chiles, and ginger. Cook for a further 5 minutes. Transfer to a sterilized jar and seal.

soy and ginger sauce

Soy and ginger make a great accompaniment to foods such as rice and vegetables that need extra seasoning. This sauce is best used within a few hours of making.

¼ cup light soy sauce

¼ cup dark soy sauce

2 inches fresh ginger, peeled and grated

1–2 tablespoons Shao Hsing (Chinese rice wine) or dry sherry (optional)

Makes about ½ cup

Mix all the ingredients in a small bowl, then serve.

plum sauce

Though spicy, this sauce isn't hot. It goes wonderfully with meaty dim sum and keeps for months in sterilized jars.

2 lb. plums, quartered and pitted

1 ¼ cups brown sugar

1 tablespoon Szechuan peppercorns, pan-toasted

1 tablespoon fennel seeds, pan-toasted

1 teaspoon whole cloves

2–3 whole star anise

1 cinnamon stick, crushed

2 inches fresh ginger, peeled and grated

1⅔ cups white rice vinegar

3 half-pint canning jars with lids, sterilized

Makes 3 cups

Put all the ingredients in a large saucepan and bring to a boil, stirring. Reduce to a steady simmer and cook for 20 minutes until the plums have broken down.

Press through a strainer to remove the spices and plum skins. Pour into sterilized jars and seal.

sweet and sour sesame sauce

This sauce will keep for up to a month in a sterilized jar—sprinkle with sesame seeds just before serving.

½ cup sugar

½ cup white rice vinegar

juice and grated zest of 1 lime

1–2 teaspoons dried chile flakes

1 tablespoon sesame seeds, toasted

Makes ½ cup

Put the sugar, vinegar, lime juice and zest, and chile flakes in a medium saucepan and bring to a boil, stirring. Simmer for 5 minutes or until reduced by half. Let cool, then pour into a serving bowl and sprinkle with the sesame seeds.

dips and sauces

index

conversion chart

Weights and measures have been rounded up
or down slightly to make measuring easier.

VOLUME EQUIVALENTS:

American	Metric	Imperial
1 teaspoon	5 ml	
1 tablespoon	15 ml	
¼ cup	60 ml	2 fl. oz.
⅓ cup	75 ml	2½ fl. oz.
½ cup	125 ml	4 fl. oz.
⅔ cup	150 ml	5 fl. oz. (¼ pint)
¾ cup	175 ml	6 fl. oz.
1 cup	250 ml	8 fl. oz.

WEIGHT EQUIVALENTS:

Imperial	Metric
1 oz.	25 g
2 oz.	50 g
3 oz.	75 g
4 oz.	125 g
5 oz.	150 g
6 oz.	175 g
7 oz.	200 g
8 oz. (½ lb.)	250 g
9 oz.	275 g
10 oz.	300 g
11 oz.	325 g
12 oz.	375 g
13 oz.	400 g
14 oz.	425 g
15 oz.	475 g
16 oz. (1 lb.)	500 g
2 lb.	1 kg

MEASUREMENTS:

Inches	Cm
¼ inch	5 mm
½ inch	1 cm
¾ inch	1.5 cm
1 inch	2.5 cm
2 inches	5 cm
3 inches	7 cm
4 inches	10 cm
5 inches	12 cm
6 inches	15 cm
7 inches	18 cm
8 inches	20 cm
9 inches	23 cm
10 inches	25 cm
11 inches	28 cm
12 inches	30 cm

OVEN TEMPERATURES:

110°C	(225°F)	Gas ¼
120°C	(250°F)	Gas ½
140°C	(275°F)	Gas 1
150°C	(300°F)	Gas 2
160°C	(325°F)	Gas 3
180°C	(350°F)	Gas 4
190°C	(375°F)	Gas 5
200°C	(400°F)	Gas 6
220°C	(425°F)	Gas 7
230°C	(450°F)	Gas 8
240°C	(475°F)	Gas 9